Sunbelly

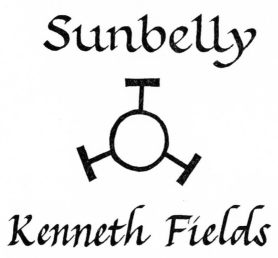

Kenneth Fields

David R. Godine

FOR ERIKA MARIA
who likes the red-tailed hawk

David R. Godine Publisher
Boston, Massachusetts

Copyright © 1973 by Kenneth Fields

LCC 73-81066
ISBN 0-87923-078-9

'Mule Deer' first appeared, under another title, in the
New Mexico Quarterly.

Designed by Carol Shloss

Number 2 in the
FIRST GODINE POETRY
CHAPBOOK SERIES

Jan Schreiber, General Editor

Blues

Red Mountain

Young girls, like wine, will be the death of me.
Non-vintage, easy, steady quantity,
The stuff I drink. I shun my proper line:
The failing, unremarkable '39.

Altamont

Paint it Black, you devils – ANON.

What were those demons playing in that din?
How could he guess? for he was up there too.
But when he felt the break and he was in,
He played more changes than he ever knew.

This was a monster group, all in his head,
All renaissance grotesques electrified,
Rats in the skull, and vultures after dead,
Buzzards of feed-back, circling, inside.

Driving, or driving hard to drive them out,
He was both band and audience. The shock –
A perfect cut down to the final shout,
Etched as in acid, perfect killer rock.

Balls

He never dreams of love, never of others,
Not even of his lovers. He is love
Centered below the navel. And above
His smile floats cool and inward. No one bothers

That constant bursting energy, flowering
Bright blossoms, blood-red hair around his head.
There is no bird is not drawn to his bed,
Though no one knows who calls and who is following.

Least of all him. He draws and he is drawn,
Beauty mirroring beauty. For this is
Reflection now, the predatory bliss,
The real sun breaking as he dreams the dawn.

Blues

Do you wait a change of weather to be gone?
I know of men who never get away,
    Who never really stay,
Homeless, but never up to moving on.

And then there are the drifters, men that comb
Through every part of country like a rain;
    Missing yet always shunning home,
Coming and lighting out on the same train.

The same train for both sorts, for whom the night
Nurses the heart in its old secret pride:
    Missing the Midnight Special's light,
Its long slow whistle down the mountainside.

Two-bits

Heavy

My name is Mud. Water and earth
Conspired to sink me at my birth.

Epitaph

He never came to spring, he went instead
After so many falls, this maiden head.

The Old Country

Daincin and drinkin, an occasional fight,
And gettin laid. Hotdamn, Saturday night.

Literalist

This innocent was ruined for a cause,
Trying to cut his teeth upon old saws.

Helpmeet

She was his much-rubbed palimpsest. Her maxim
Was *He for books, and she for books in him.*

Biog.

Poets are known by readers and by lovers:
Discreet, separate but equal under covers.

Visionary

It's not because he likes it, but to see
If he can do it, that he screws so many,
Drops in for coffee, solace, and a roll,
Shedding distinction easily with his clothes;
Then leaves abstracted, *each* as good as *any*,
Passion, like ether, pure to the pure soul.

Punch-Drunk

It's now or never. Well, how many times,
Trying to find a center in the weather,
Had he found instead unseasonable emptiness? –
In rain or sun, the still coldwave of boredom?
That's what he got from drinking: a *now* that was
Never: the straight-shot drop, the cold-cock knockout.

Boss

All night he heard the sound of mountain water,
The clear streams of the past falling away
From a lake in the high country. The black ducks there
And rainbows would be rising with the sun
But not for him. It was already over.
It was already dawn and he let it be.
He knew without looking that the world was gone,
The frogs hoarse in the reeds about the edges,
And in its place this ringing in his ears –
After which, nothing, which was what he wanted.
It was a kind of truth, the brutal Boss.

Search Party

Men will be coming with the first spring thaw
To puzzle over the pieces drifted away:
The trailing edge of a wing, the scattered body,

The bodies, then even the dream-like snowdrifts
Gone into earth and air. What will they make
Of the shards of life up there on Memory Ridge? –

Of the strange journals kept by one or two?
' *Today the bacon's gone. I tried to sleep ...*
The snow is falling out of the air like light.'

Juan Songs

Paths

Smoother
Than mountains seen
Through the pale distance,
Their steep sides,
The slides
Of blue shale, certainly
Certainly there.
But they cannot
Be seen.

Mule Deer

Brownshirt's eye
Along his arrow.
Now through the brush
It goes whistling behind me.

Red-tailed Hawk

Ha! What a fine trick!
Shifting a little in the air
I trap the great winds
Blowing me here and there
All over the earth!

Wind

Whorls in the tips of my fingers
Moving
Over the land.

Warrior

Floating at noon, red-tailed hawks in the air
Circling the sun: striking, I am not here.

Water

Everything is here.
Wait a little. The bottom
Is Mexico, Arizona, is shifting.

Weeds
Reach toward light, while the light
Pulls
At the surfaces, now and now —
Trees, sky, the muzzles of small animals, the sun:

The eye
That could not see the sun
If it were not
Itself the sun. Or water.
It is. It is.

Magpie

Black hair, the hair of animals at night,
Manes of black ponies, a white blaze on each forehead,
White pollen above each running hoof,
A black wind lifting above each running flower:
So she herself comes walking, the Magpie-Woman,
Full of herself, she comes
Walking, her power in the corners of her eyes.

Canyon

My dreams are red feathers
And stone, drifting
And falling. Only this morning
Before the first light, I saw
That I would be that hawk I think I am:
I would go up
Soaring and hovering, a new sun
Up over the rim of that old canyon,
And I would drop,
The centuries rushing in my wings,
Down to the Red Snake Twisting Along The Gorge,
To you, beautiful Magpie,
Beautiful Bird Always Floating Away.

Great Wind

You, who cannot make up your mind!
I come from the north,
Rushing around, whirling away the dust.
You, who cannot make up your mind,
I come from the north, woman.
What are you waiting for!

Sunbelly

Something Looking for Me

In my mind I am always making journeys.
Walking out through the hills,
Turning over rocks, noting
A burst of lupine, or the angle
A dove makes taking its branch.
Is it here? Where will I find it?
Then only the light, the silence
Composing itself around me,
Singing and filling up
Everywhere at once like sound.

The Satellite Lover

He hears whining.
He does not know what it means.
Over and over again,
It is the same tune.
Moving his hands or feet
Or finally his head
Does not help.
He does not even know it
When it comes to get him.

Red Wing

By water and by air you come, red-shouldered,
Large as a woman, moving like a fish

Down through the trees, gills and fins and feathers
Breathing, touching, and floating in the leaves.

Loop

It is an old design.
Entering into itself
The self is lost:
The same each time,
Emptiness turning in a single line.

Imperative

Quiet and darkness. Let it all rush in!
There is a hush beyond the edge of things
That you may catch by letting go. Leave off
Following the old sun for a little while.
Within, there is another; to the source
A quiet brother, humming as you hum.
It was for this that you found what you found,
Sun of the belly, perfect, webbed, and round.

On Ahead

Grown thinner every day, the shadows stealing
Your flesh so slowly that we could not follow,
You sailed into pure self in those last weeks,
The body luffing, lines gone in the dark air;
Out to the light, in to the bright center,
You were subsiding back into the wind
From which god spoke the word. I saw you out,
Catching only in nightmares the last breath.
Now standing in your orchard four years later,
Your peace settling like light in the light rain,
I hear your voice clearer than winter sun:
The last few days, I have been almost lucent.
And now you are. Beautiful. Lucent. Alive.

Notes

'Boss' is about Ernest Hemingway, and was inspired by Carlos Baker's great biography. See especially the last two pages. Hemingway killed himself with one of his favorite weapons, a Boss shotgun. For the second half of the first line I owe an unconscious debt to Wallace Stegner.

The Juan Songs are influenced by American Indian poems and ways of thinking and dealing with the world. The title refers to the great Yaqui wise man and teacher, the *brujo* Don Juan, hero of the three books by Carlos Castaneda. Most of the poems celebrate totems.

After I had given my book its title and organization and after I had written 'Imperative', a friend showed me the following statement by Picasso: 'When you come right down to it all you have is yourself. Yourself is a sun with a thousand rays in your belly. The rest is nothing. It is only because of this that Picasso is Picasso. It is because I carry the sun in my belly that I can accomplish something from time to time.'